30-Point Plan To Winning Your Employees' Loyalty And Respect

By Levon Sparks Salone

Kindle Edition 2014

Copyright©2014 Levon Sparks Salone

All rights reserved. No part of this book may be used or reproduced in any manner without written permission of the author/publisher, except in the case of brief quotations embodied in reviews.

Other Books by Levon Sparks Salone

Fiction:

Waltzing With Deception (The Chillings Series, Book 1)

Unjust Ruling (The Chillings Series, Book 2)

Non-Fiction:

Men Hurt Too!

Writing Prompts For Creative Writers

150 Plus 1 Acts of Kindness

Introduction

Let's face it...employees are valuable assets to your company. It is more beneficial to keep valuable employees for extended periods of time rather than training new employees month after month. By keeping well-trained employees on your team, you can save thousands of dollars and raise the productivity in your company.

One way to keep well-trained employees is to help them develop loyalty and respect for your company. How can you do this? By showing <u>them</u> loyalty and respect. Sounds simple? Well, it works!

In this manual, ***30-Point Plan To Winning Your Employees' Loyalty And Respect***, the author shows you how to help your employees develop commitment to your company. If you desire to see the level of productivity rise within your company, begin applying these success-proven strategies.

Companies that remain on the cutting edge have learned how to implement these strategies effectively. Be among the best...let your employees know they are important, and they will help you and your company soar to higher heights.

Success Principle 1

Give a hand-written note to an employee voicing your appreciation for his or her hard work. (Either call him or her into your office or leave the note at his or her workstation.)

The Power Of A Hand-written Note

It shows that you recognized your employee did something well.

After the recognition, you took personal time out of your schedule to acknowledge the accomplishment.

It provides the employee with something tangible and concrete...something they can read repeatedly.

It affirms the employee.

It's inexpensive, yet effective.

Did you know that many employers have never written an employee a thank-you note?

You may be surprised, but practicing this step can thrust you on the cutting edge and assist you in developing stronger employer-employee relationships.

Success Principle 2

Choose a day to buy lunch for your employees. If you are a large business, you can purchase lunch for one department at a time.

The Power Of Lunch Buying

Important Note: Everyone has to eat!

...And one way that an employer can show appreciation for his/her employees is to buy them lunch. This does not have to be an expensive gesture, but it is a way to celebrate your employees' accomplishments. Remember, your ultimate goal is to reinforce positive behavior. Applying this tool will be extremely inexpensive yet it can produce results that will be far-reaching.

Success Principle 3

Verbally let your employees know that they are doing good jobs. Visit them at their workstations and tell them you like what you see.

The Power Of A Verbal "Thank-You"

One of the major complaints among employees is they believe no one in management appreciates what they do. Some say they pour their minds, abilities and even their lives into someone else's company without a mere "thank-you." Surprisingly, many employees are motivated by spoken words; thus, validating the power of the verbal "thank-you."

Advantages of this concept:
It's free to implement.

It helps to curtail the complaint that no one in management recognizes employees' efforts.

*It **immediately** affirms employees.*

The use of this tool can validate your employee's accomplishments or his/her presence.

Bob, thank you for completing that report on time.

Cindy, thank you for choosing to work at this company; it is a pleasure having you on board.

Success Principle 4

Post names of exceptional employees on bulletin boards or in newsletters at your company.

People like recognition for the things they've done well. If you have employees who have risen to the occasion to get your company's goals accomplished, you should display them, like valued trophies.

The Power Of Recognizing Exceptional Employees

It allows employees to know they are above average, and you have recognized it.

It causes these employees' peers to recognize them.

It provides other employees with examples of behaviors you consider to be above the norm.

It gives other employees obtainable goals to reach.

The use of this strategy can motivate other employees. Sometimes the thought of recognition spurs others to action.

Success Principle 5

Give an employee an extra hour for lunch, allow him/her to leave one hour early or come in one hour late (with pay). Tell him/her it's just a small token of appreciation for a job well done. (You can extend the period to 2 hours, 3 hours, 1/2 day, etc.)

The Power Of Extra Time Off
(With Pay)

Giving an employee extra time away from his/her workplace is an excellent way for an employer to say that he/she appreciates his/her employee's efforts. There is something notable about an employer who gives his/her employee extra time away from the workplace to do something he/she enjoys or needs to do. This is especially beneficial if the employer compensates the worker for that time. Not only is this an excellent re-enforcer, it can also help motivate employees to work harder to get that extra time off; thereby, assisting in alleviating requests to take a longer lunch or come into the workplace later.

Employers can reward employees with this time off and tell them to use it when needed.

Success Principle 6

Give a gift certificate to a popular store in your area. (You can have a suggestion box allowing your employees to list places they enjoy shopping.)

There is an ancient principle that states that your gift will make room for you. Not only is it referring to one's abilities and talents, but it is also referring to one's ability to give to another freely.

The business world underutilizes this concept. Finding out what an employee likes and purchasing those small tokens of appreciation for a job well done help to develop a sense of loyalty for an employee.

The Power Of The Gift Certificate

The employee has some input regarding his/her reward.

As an employer, you acknowledged that you heard the request, and you followed through with action.

Success Principle 7

Have a special parking space for the employee of the month.

You can honor an employee for a month by using this strategy. It tells the employee as well as others that he/she was appreciated for his/her overall performance.

If possible, this parking space should be located close to the entrance of the workplace, signifying a sense of status.

The Underlying Message Of This Strategy

This is a way to say "thank-you" to an employee for an entire month without having to repeat it with words.

Success Principle 8

Give your employees opportunities to have breakfast or lunch with you on a quarterly basis.

The Power Of Your Presence

Many employers stay aloof from their employees. However, studies show that relationships move people, especially females. By implementing this strategy into your arsenal, you will get to know those who work for you, and it allows them to get to know you. Developing positive relationships (even though not intimate) can be a positive enhancer in the workplace.

Success Principle 9

Have monthly or quarterly luncheons for new employees. Honor new employees at these luncheons and tell them you appreciate them coming aboard.

The Power Behind This Strategy

This strategy shows a newcomer that you appreciate his/her making the decision to come work with your company. It starts him/her off with positive affirmations. This alone can raise the morale and productivity in the workplace.

Success Principle 10

Have a suggestion box so that employees can suggest areas of improvement for your company.

The Power Behind This Strategy

Many employers overlook great suggestions that their employees may have. Everyone has a different perspective about things, and utilizing some of your employees' ideas can boost the effectiveness of your company.

(Note: The best employers are the ones who know how to utilize all of his/her resources.)

Success Principle 11

Run a contest identifying the most creative way to save your company money. Give a prize and company recognition to the winner.

The Power Of The Contest

This strategy draws the creativity out of your employees.

It helps your employees remain energized by creating healthy competition.

Ideas produced as a result of this contest can move your business on the cutting edge.

Important Reminders:

Some employees have areas of expertise that the employer doesn't have. Getting feedback from them can help perfect something that is good or help change an old, out-dated system.

Make sure that the prize awarded will be something that's beneficial to your employee.

Success Principle 12

Have a company picnic one time per year. Allow employees to invite their families to this function.

The Power Of The Company Picnic

This strategy allows you to get to know your employees outside of the workplace.

It's a way to say "thank-you" and have fun in the process.

(For an added incentive, coordinate team-building exercises during this event. This can help your employees with bonding and help them develop a sense of loyalty to you and your company.)

Success Principle 13

Have an awards banquet and recognize the accomplishments of your employees.

This strategy can be a formal or an informal event. Companies usually host this event once a year.

(Note: This technique may be more time consuming and costly than some of the other techniques listed, but if your company can afford to do this, it is an excellent way to tell your employees that you appreciate them and their efforts.)

Success Principle 14

Give a bonus check once or twice a year. You can give the same amount across the board or give on a percentage basis.

The Underlying Message Of This Strategy

For some people, money is always a motivator. As an employer, you cannot go wrong using this strategy.

Caution!!!

When using this strategy, you must consider your company's budget. If you can't afford to give yearly bonuses, you have several options:

Give bonuses based on time of employment (after 2 years, 5 years, 7 years, etc.).

Give bonuses to all of your employees every second or third year.

Give bonuses based on goals met instead of time employed with company.

Success Principle 15

Give employees gifts with your company logo on them.

The Power Behind This Strategy

Not only is this an inexpensive way to show appreciation for your employees, but it is a great marketing tool for your company. By doing a little research, you can find items that range from a few dollars to more elaborate prices. If you are cost conscious, buying in bulk will also help decrease some of your costs.

Brief list of suggestions:

Coffee mugs

T-shirts

Pencils and Pens

Key Rings

Caps

Stress Balls

Calendars

Letter Openers

Notebooks

Totes

Success Principle 16

Pay for your employees' trainings, courses, etc. if they will enhance your employees' skills to perform their jobs more effectively. (You can pay a percentage or the total amount of the classes.)

The Rationale Behind This Strategy

Companies tend to lag behind if they fail to keep their employees abreast of the new developments in their fields. It is essential that you use this strategy if you desire to remain on the cutting edge. Even if you can't afford to send your employees to major conferences and pay for all of their travel arrangements, you have the option of bringing individuals onto your site to train your employees on critical skills that are essential for your company's continual advancement. Some companies err in that they only send management to trainings; thus, failing to educate other laborers, leaving them in stagnant positions.

Success Principle 17

Give your employees raises (a small raise is better than no raise).

The Rationale Behind This Strategy

Not many employees will refuse additional money. Money can serve as a powerful motivator.

Note: This strategy will be contingent upon your company's budget.

Success Principle 18

Give out plaques monthly or quarterly for exceptional employees.

The Power Of Giving Plaques

It gives employees something tangible to display. (Some employees like to display plaques, indicating their business savvy.)

It produces healthy competition in the work environment.

It is not extremely costly, but some employees see it as having more prestige than a hand-written note.

Success Principle 19

If your employee comes to you with a complaint, allow him/her to be a part of the problem-solving process. Ask him/her to give suggestions for improvements.

The Rationale Behind This Strategy

If allowed the opportunity, many employees have answers on how to solve conflict in the workplace. By making them a part of the problem-solving process, the employer is taking some of the responsibility off him/her and placing it onto them. This process will also help eliminate individuals coming to you who just want to complain without making any changes.

Success Principle 20

Recognize each employee's birthday with a free lunch (or other small token of appreciation).

The Rationale Behind This Strategy

This strategy allows the employer to tell an employee that his/her birthday is special. It may seem like a small token, but acknowledging an employee on his/her birthday can be a great way to validate the person instead of his/her accomplishments.

Success Principle 21

Allow employees to post significant events in your company's newsletter (births of children, graduations, weddings, etc.). If you don't have a newsletter, this would be an excellent time to start one.

The Rationale Behind This Strategy

Many employees like to share positive things about their families. If an employer provides an avenue for this to happen, he/she is saying that those who are important to his/her employees are important to him/her. It is a way to spread cheer throughout the work environment.

Success Principle 22

Bring in trainers to teach employees how to perform their jobs more proficiently. If available, use trainer from within your company.

The Rationale Behind This Strategy

This is an excellent way to train your employees yet keep costs down. It is more beneficial to have someone come into your facility to train your employees, paying the trainer one set fee, versus sending all of your employees out to a training.

If you elect to use trainers from within your organization, you can shave costs even more.

Benefits Of Using Trainers From Within Your Organization:

It gives a sense of esteem to the trainer.

It allows someone who is familiar with your organization to address issues from that vantage point.

Caution!!!

At times, it may be better to use someone outside of your organization. They may be able to present information more objectively.

Success Principle 23

Give away a weekend for two to the exceptional employee. This can be as simple as sending him/her to a bed and breakfast in your local area.

The Rationale Behind This Strategy

Using this strategy may be more costly, but it can provide a stress-reliever for an employee. The ultimate goal is to provide an outlet for the employee because of a job well done.

(Note: A bed and breakfast may offer your company a discount if you share that you will be using its services frequently.)

Success Principle 24

Have staff meetings where employees can share their work-related concerns. The first half of each meeting is for identifying concerns; the second half is for finding solutions.

The Power Of Staff Meetings

They keep the lines of communication open between employer and employee.

They keep the lines of communication open between employee and employee.

If anyone brings up a concern, he/she is also required to bring up a <u>possible</u> solution.

This tool allows the employer to keep abreast of issues that need immediate attention.

Success Principle 25

When conflicts arise, address them immediately.

The Rationale Behind This Strategy

The old adage one bad apple can spoil the whole bunch is definitely true. When conflict arises within an organization, an employer must have steps in place to address the conflict immediately. Failure to do so can produce an atmosphere of negativity thereby significantly decreasing the morale and productivity in your organization.

Success Principle 26

Make sure you have an effective way to communicate your company's policies and procedures to your employees. When your company implements a new policy or procedure, you may need to post the new policy or procedure in a staff area for at least a week (in addition to being included in your policy and procedure manual).

The Rationale Behind This Strategy

This tool keeps your employees updated on your company's policies and procedures. By posting policies and procedures in staff areas for a short period, the employer is reinforcing/reminding employees of necessary changes.

Suggestion: *Request that your employees sporadically review your policy and procedure manual.*

Success Principle 27

Provide as many employee benefits as possible (health insurance, vacation pay, etc.).

The Rationale Behind This Strategy

This strategy shows your employees that you care about their total well-being (physical, recreational, etc.). Employee Assistance Programs (EAPs) are excellent for helping employees deal with personal issues that may be interfering with their job performances.

Success Principle 28

Give your employees discounts on the products your company offers.

Two Benefits Of This Strategy

It helps the employee save money.

It serves as an advertising tool for your company.

(Note: Others seeing your employees with your clothing, furnishings, cars, etc. may be prone to purchase them from you also.)

Success Principle 29

Bring in temporary staff to assist with duties if your regular employees are overworked. (Duties temporary staff can perform are answering telephones, filing or keeping work area clean. Ask employees how temporary staff can assist them.)

The Rationale Behind This Strategy

This strategy can reduce your regular employees' workloads; thereby, alleviating some of their stress. An employer can hire individuals from temporary services and use them as long as they desire. This will free your regular employees to perform other aspects of their jobs.

(You can use interns and volunteers in this capacity.)

Success Principle 30

Keep your word when dealing with your employees. If you tell them you are going to do something, do it!

Employer Note Sheet

Employer Note Sheet

www.ingramcontent.com/pod-product-compliance
Lightning Source LLC
Chambersburg PA
CBHW070728180526
45167CB00004B/1662